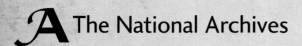
The National Archives

SHAKESPEARE

UNCLASSIFIED

Secrets of the Great Bard of Avon Revealed

The Globe

BY NICK HUNTER

A & C BLACK
AN IMPRINT OF BLOOMSBURY
LONDON   OXFORD   NEW DELHI   NEW YORK   SYDNEY

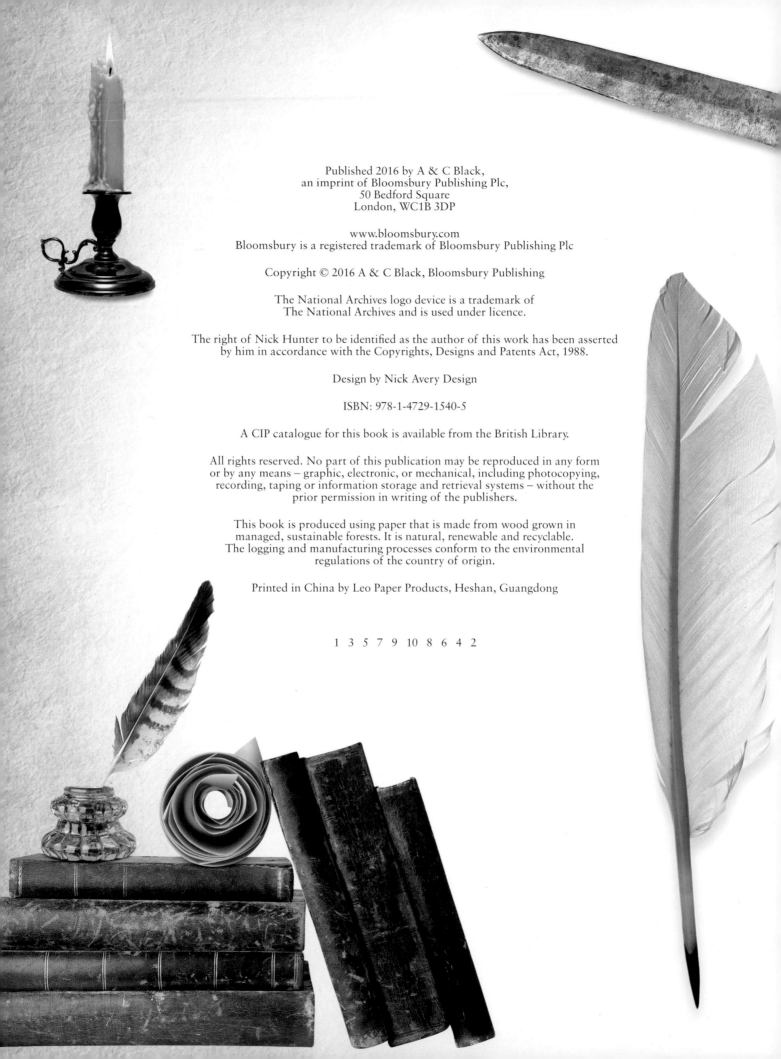

Published 2016 by A & C Black,
an imprint of Bloomsbury Publishing Plc,
50 Bedford Square
London, WC1B 3DP

www.bloomsbury.com
Bloomsbury is a registered trademark of Bloomsbury Publishing Plc

Copyright © 2016 A & C Black, Bloomsbury Publishing

The National Archives logo device is a trademark of
The National Archives and is used under licence.

The right of Nick Hunter to be identified as the author of this work has been asserted
by him in accordance with the Copyrights, Designs and Patents Act, 1988.

Design by Nick Avery Design

ISBN: 978-1-4729-1540-5

A CIP catalogue for this book is available from the British Library.

This book is produced using paper that is made from wood grown in
managed, sustainable forests. It is natural, renewable and recyclable.
The logging and manufacturing processes conform to the environmental
regulations of the country of origin.

Printed in China by Leo Paper Products, Heshan, Guangdong

1 3 5 7 9 10 8 6 4 2

CONTENTS

A NEW STAGE

In spring 1599, visitors to the crime-infested taverns and bear-baiting arenas of London's Bankside would have seen a new building rising above the filthy, crowded streets. Word spread that this building, called the Globe Theatre, was the new home of the Lord Chamberlain's Men.

▲ *The mysterious William Shakespeare.*

The Lord Chamberlain's Men were one of London's leading groups of actors. These talented performers could entertain their audiences with hilarious comedy or shock them with heart-breaking tragedy. The secret to their success lay with the person who wrote their plays; a young man from rural Warwickshire who would become the most brilliant playwright of his time. His name was William Shakespeare.

▲ *Signatures like this one, on his will, are the only definite examples we have of Shakespeare's own handwriting.*

Risky Profession

Shakespeare and his partners had a lot riding on the success of the Globe Theatre. Earning a living as an actor and playwright during the reign of Elizabeth I was tough. An outbreak of plague could close the theatres for months or even years. If a play offended the wrong person, they could end up in prison, or murdered like Shakespeare's rival, Christopher Marlowe.

▲ *The theatres of Tudor London were remembered in a series of postage stamps (1995), such as this stamp of the Swan Theatre.*

◀ *Theatres had to compete with other popular entertainments, such as bear baiting, in which a bear was attacked by dogs.*

▲ *Shakespeare grew up in the country, where he may have been inspired by a travelling group of actors.*

How did a boy from a country town, with a basic grammar-school education, create some of the world's greatest poetry and plays? This book uses documents from Shakespeare's life to piece together his story and to try and explain how William Shakespeare became the greatest writer of his age, or any other.

▶ *London's theatres were popular with people from all levels of society.*

"Oh how the audience Were ravished, with what wonder they went home."
Audiences were entranced by Shakespeare's Julius Caesar, as this short review shows.

WHO WAS WILLIAM SHAKESPEARE?

William Shakespeare has been famous for so long that it is amazing how little we actually know about him. We know a child of that name was born in Stratford-upon-Avon, Warwickshire, in April 1564. We know when he died and various documents give us a glimpse of Shakespeare's life in Stratford and London. But there is so much that we cannot be sure about.

▲ *This entry in the parish register records the baptism of Shakespeare on Wednesday 26 April 1564.*

What did Shakespeare look like?

There is one surviving portrait of Shakespeare that was probably painted in his lifetime, but experts can't be sure that it does in fact show Shakespeare. An engraving in the first collection of Shakespeare's plays and the memorial statue in Stratford church both appeared after his death, although people who knew the playwright were still alive to complain if they did not look like him. Every picture since has been based on one of these portraits.

▲ *If this portrait does show the face of William Shakespeare, it is probably the only likeness we have that was painted during his lifetime.*

What did he write?

We may not be certain what he looked like, but at least we have Shakespeare's words; or do we? His plays and poems include around a million words, but we only have 14 words in Shakespeare's own handwriting, and 12 of them are examples of his signature. In each of those signature examples, Shakespeare, Shakspere or Shakespe, spells his name differently.

Some experts even think that Shakespeare's plays were written by someone else, but we'll come back to that later.

▲ *Official documents tell us that this house was where Shakespeare's mother, Mary Arden, grew up.*

▼ *Seven years after his death, two of Shakespeare's fellow actors published 36 of his plays in this book, called the* First Folio.

To the Reader.
This Figure, that thou here seest put,
It was for gentle Shakespeare cut;
Wherein the Grauer had a strife
with Nature, to out-doo the life:
O, could he but haue drawne his wit
As well in brasse, as he hath hit
His face; the Print would then surpasse
All, that was euer writ in brasse.
But, since he cannot, Reader, looke
Not on his Picture, but his Booke.
B. I.

Mr. WILLIAM
SHAKESPEARES
COMEDIES,
HISTORIES, &
TRAGEDIES.
Published according to the True Originall Copies.

LONDON
Printed by Isaac Iaggard, and Ed. Blount. 1623.

▲ *Memorial to Shakespeare in his home town of Stratford-upon-Avon.*

COUNTRY BOY

Shakespeare's story begins in the small town of Stratford-upon-Avon, Warwickshire, where he was born in April 1564. Stratford was a prosperous country town and Shakespeare's father, John Shakespeare, was one of the leading citizens.

John Shakespeare was elected to many important jobs in the town, including high bailiff, or mayor, in 1568. He worked as a glove-maker, creating fashionable and expensive gloves from white leather. This was a very respectable trade. Shakespeare's mother, Mary, was the daughter of a local farmer. He was the third of eight children, although his elder brother and sister died before he was born.

Plague comes to Stratford

Shakespeare was quite lucky to survive childhood at all. Three months after his birth, Stratford was hit by the plague. In just a few months, this deadly outbreak wiped out one-tenth of the town's population, including a family of four in Henley Street, where the Shakespeare family lived.

Shakespeare's birthday

Shakespeare's birthday is celebrated on 23 April, which is also St George's Day, which remembers the patron saint of England. No one can be sure that this was actually his birthday. However, he was certainly baptized three days later, which was normal at the time as one in five babies died before they were a month old.

◀ The ornate leather gloves made by John Shakespeare would have been the height of fashion for Stratford's leading families.

▲ William Shakespeare was born in this house on Henley Street, which was also his father's workshop.

▼ Shakespeare and his friends played with simple homemade toys and games.

▲ This document is the earliest evidence that John Shakespeare lived in Stratford. In 1552, he was fined for making a refuse heap in Henley Street. All kinds of human and animal waste could be found in Tudor streets, and John Shakespeare may have been using this waste for the smelly process of softening leather.

A Tudor Education

Growing up in a small town such as Stratford meant that Shakespeare had the chance to go to school, unlike many children at the time. He would have been sent to 'petty' school from about the age of five, where he learned the alphabet.

▲ *Hornbooks like this were used to teach the alphabet.*

At the age of about seven, Shakespeare went to Stratford's grammar school along with the other sons of the town's most prominent families. There is no written proof of this but it would have been unusual for the son of a leading citizen not to attend school. The school day began very early and there were few holidays.

▼ *Life was hard for Tudor schoolboys, who were beaten by their teachers for the smallest offence.*

The grammar school taught Shakespeare many things that he would use in later life, but the boy who would become the greatest English writer was not taught in English. Most lessons were in Latin and the plays and poetry Shakespeare studied would have been in Latin too. Latin was an international language and knowing how to read it enabled young people, like Shakespeare, to read the works of writers from across Europe.

Playing and players

When he was not at school, Shakespeare would have played games with his friends, such as a rough version of football. The main days to relax were religious holidays, when local people would put on plays, usually of scenes from the Bible. The young Shakespeare may also have been inspired by travelling acting troupes, which sometimes visited the town.

◀ The plays Shakespeare discovered at school would have been in Latin and once performed by Roman actors.

▲ In Shakespeare's time, around 40 boys would have been taught in the schoolroom of the King's New School in Stratford-upon-Avon.

"I have been told ... by some of the neighbours, that when he was a boy he exercised his father's trade, but when he killed a calf, he would do it in a high style, and make a speech."

John Aubrey, writing long after Shakespeare's death, suggests that Shakespeare was an actor, even as a child.

▶ Queen Elizabeth I allowed her subjects to read the Bible in English, which had been banned by her sister Queen Mary, who died in 1558.

TUDOR TURMOIL

William Shakespeare was growing up at a time when English society was in turmoil. Queen Elizabeth I came to the throne six years before Shakespeare was born. For many years, England had been torn apart by religious divisions after Elizabeth's father, Henry VIII, had left the Roman Catholic Church and declared himself head of a new Church of England.

Queen Mary, Elizabeth's sister, had tried to reverse this change. Bitter divisions between Catholics and Protestants continued throughout Elizabeth's, and Shakespeare's, life. Changes in society went beyond religion. During the 1500s, explorers and seafarers discovered and traded with many new lands. The known world now extended to the Americas and East Asia. The first printing press had been set up less than a century before, and new printed books spread ideas and knowledge to anyone who could read. For the teenage Shakespeare, Stratford must have started to seem like a very small corner of the world.

▲ *The changes during Elizabeth I's reign were vital to Shakespeare's success.*

▼ *In the reign of Henry VIII, most plays dealt with religious subjects.*

Theatre revolution

Elizabeth's reign was also a time of revolution in the theatre. Previously, most plays had been religious stories, but these had been banned along with the Roman Catholic religion. There was room for new types of play and William Shakespeare would arrive on stage at just the right time.

◀ *Catholic religious objects, such as rosary beads, were forbidden during Elizabeth's reign.*

▼ This map shows Roanoke Island, in what is now North Carolina, USA. It was created in 1585 and is perhaps the first English map of North America made by people who had actually been there.

Caca Fogo.

Caca Plata.

▲ Ships and seafarers feature in many of Shakespeare's plays. Their stories of new lands and perilous journeys must have fired his imagination.

▼ If the printing press had not been invented, Shakespeare's plays would not have been widely available.

▲ This document was printed on William Caxton's new printing press in 1476.

FAMILY MYSTERIES

The 1570s were difficult times for the Shakespeare family. John, who had been a leading figure in the town, was taken to court for lending money and for trading wool.

Whether he was guilty or not, John Shakespeare stopped attending council meetings and he seems to have taken no part in public life after 1576, when his eldest son was 12. William Shakespeare left school around the age of 15. The early years of his working life are a mystery, but his personal life was soon turned upside down.

Marriage and family

In November 1582, when Shakespeare was only 18, he married Anne Hathaway, who was eight years older. The marriage seems to have taken place in a hurry and it wasn't long before the couple's first child Susanna was born in May 1583. Twins Hamnet and Judith arrived in 1585.

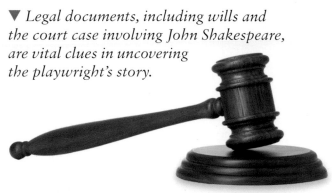

▼ Legal documents, including wills and the court case involving John Shakespeare, are vital clues in uncovering the playwright's story.

◀ This portrait may show Anne Hathaway. It was drawn many years later but could be a copy of an Elizabethan picture.

◀ The will of Anne Hathaway's father Richard, who died in 1582, shows that she came from a family of prosperous farmers.

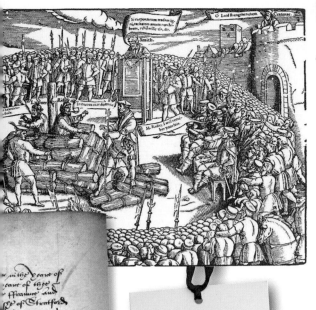

Were Shakespeare's family Catholics?

The Catholic faith was illegal at this time but still widespread in Warwickshire. The list below was drawn up in 1592. It lists the people not attending Protestant church and was drawn up to try and identify secret Catholics. John Shakespeare is listed as staying away because he was in debt and did not want to be taken to court. Was this the real reason and how did the family fall on such hard times?

▲ Heretics risked being burned at the stake, although only four Catholics suffered this during Elizabeth's reign.

▼ Many young men became apprentices in their teens to learn a trade, but there is no evidence that Shakespeare took this route.

THE YOUNG WRITER

After Shakespeare's marriage to Anne, and the birth of his three children, he vanishes for several years. There are no historical records between 1585 and 1592 that can tell us where he was during this time or what he was doing.

Sometime during these years, Shakespeare moved from Stratford to London and became known as a writer, but that is all we know for sure.

Hiding in Lancashire

Some experts claim that Shakespeare spent time as a musician or performer in the house of a leading Catholic family in Lancashire. Household records mention a "William Shakeshafte". This is possible but why would Shakespeare have changed his name? If it was him, then Shakespeare lived in Lancashire just before his marriage to Anne, so it does not help much in explaining his lost years.

Travelling the world

Another theory is that Shakespeare spent these years travelling the world as a seafarer or soldier. The only evidence for this comes from the far-off settings and sea voyages that feature in many of his plays. However, Shakespeare's knowledge of the world could just as easily have been picked up in the bustling port of London.

▶ *Many young men left their homes to find success in London, but most of them did not leave behind a wife and young family, as Shakespeare did.*

Running away to the theatre?

Shakespeare would have enjoyed plays performed by bands of travelling actors when they visited Stratford. The Queen's Men performed in the town in 1587. Is it possible that Shakespeare joined them and left his home town? There is no proof of this, but it would explain how the son of a glove-maker reached the theatres of London.

▲ Shakespeare's plays often included sea voyages and great storms, but could he have been writing from experience?

◄ John Aubrey, writer (1626 – 1697), suggested that the young Shakespeare worked as a teacher.

THE BIG CITY

Today, it is an easy journey from Stratford to London. However, in Shakespeare's time it took four days on foot or two days by horse. It must have been a big decision for Shakespeare to leave his wife and young children, but if he wanted to work in the theatre he had no choice. He either had to join a travelling company of actors or try his luck in the big city.

▲ Travellers on rough muddy Tudor roads needed strong shoes and hoped for good weather.

London was much smaller than it is now in Shakespeare's time, but it was one of the biggest cities in Europe, and was home to about 200,000 people. As he entered the city for the first time, the noise, smell and bustle of its narrow streets would have been overwhelming.

Shakespeare probably arrived in the capital around the time England was under threat of invasion by the Spanish Armada of 1588. Queen Elizabeth was at the height of her popularity and there was a growing national pride in England.

Youth and talent

Life in London was tough, dirty and dangerous. On average, Londoners did not live past the age of 35. New people were constantly arriving from across England and the world. It was a youthful city and a young man with talent and ambition could certainly make a name for himself.

▶ Places of entertainment such as theatres were usually outside the city walls or in Southwark, on the south bank of the River Thames.

arundel house · Essex house · Temple stayres · Beere bayting h

LONDINVM FERACISSIMI AN-
GLIAE REGNI METROPOLIS

▲ Tudor London was four times the size in 1600 as it had been a century earlier. This map dates from 1572.

Black freyars

The Globe

Londons Charitie

Dead.

Buried

the Conntries Crueltie

▲ London was hit by regular outbreaks of the dreaded plague. In 1593, more than 14% of the population died in one outbreak.

A DAY AT THE THEATRE

For the people of London, a day at the theatre was a new experience. The Earl of Leicester's actors had started performing for the public in 1574, in the courtyard of the Bull Inn in Bishopsgate. In 1577, James Burbage opened The Theatre. This was the first building in London that was purely used for performing plays. Others soon followed.

Attending the theatre was not just a pastime for the rich and fashionable. Ordinary people flocked to see the performers too. Many theatre-goers would not have been able to read or write but for a penny they could spend an afternoon in the open air watching a play. A seat in the galleries around the edge of the theatre would cost a bit more. Theatres were noisy, dirty, and contained rich pickings for thieves and pickpockets.

▲ *Richard Tarlton was the most popular comic actor of the age.*

Putting on a show

The words of the plays may have been poetic, but the performers also had to put on a show. There was no scenery so everything depended on the skill of the actors and the quality of the play.

▼ *Real guns and ammunition were used to liven up the plays. Sometimes audience members were killed or injured by these.*

The people loved the rude jokes and misunderstandings of comedies, but they especially loved the violence of tragedies such as Thomas Kyd's *The Spanish Tragedy* or Christopher Marlowe's *Tamburlaine the Great*. Life was brutal, and the cruel tortures and bloody murders in the plays reflected this.

▲ Going to the theatre was more comfortable if you paid more money. A seat in a box cost around six pence.

tectum

porticus

mimorum ædes

orchestia

ingressus

proscænium

planties fine arena

Men only

Shakespeare and rival playwrights included parts for women in their plays, but there were no female actors before 1660. Characters like the tragic lover Juliet would have been played by young boys.

▲ This sketch of the Swan Theatre in London is the only known drawing from the time showing what the inside of an Elizabethan theatre really looked like.

ACTOR AND PLAYWRIGHT

Shakespeare's career in London probably started as an actor, and he may have travelled to the city in the first place as part of an acting company. He could even have risen from the lowly position of call-boy, whose job was to tell the actors when they were due on stage.

Actors needed training, in skills such as sword-fighting and dancing as well as making yourself heard above the din of the theatre. We know that Shakespeare appeared in several plays. However, he was never a leading actor, and probably spent most of his time writing once he and his fellow players realized the power of his pen.

Getting noticed

The first mention of Shakespeare the playwright comes in 1592, but he was almost certainly quite well known by then. Robert Greene, a fellow writer, calls him "an upstart crow" who "supposes he is as well able to bombast out a blank verse as the best of you". Greene may have been jealous or poking fun at Shakespeare's humble background, but it shows that he was getting noticed. Within a few years, Shakespeare's plays would dominate the London scene.

▲ Holinshed's Chronicles *were an important source for history plays such as* Richard III.

Sourcing or stealing?

Shakespeare did not usually make up the stories in his plays. He borrowed characters, plots and even words from lots of different sources. These included *Holinshed's Chronicles*, published in 1587 and the main source for Shakespeare's history plays, and Arthur Brooke's poem *The Tragical History of Romeo and Juliet*. Most writers at the time did the same.

▲ *Shakespeare may have started his career performing outside taverns.*

▼ *The tragedy* King Lear *was based on a mixture of history and legend about Britain's past.*

"THE PLAY'S THE THING..."

Shakespeare wrote at least 37 plays. He may have worked with another writer on some of them and there are probably other plays that have not survived. On average, he wrote one or two plays every year, but this work rate was not unusual. Thomas Heywood, writing around the same time, claimed to have written more than 200 plays in his career.

Shakespeare's plays show a huge variety. He wrote at least 17 comedies, 10 history plays and 10 tragedies. Their lengths varied dramatically, with the tragedy *Hamlet* being the longest with more than 4,000 lines. Most were written in unrhyming, or blank, verse but also included scenes written in prose.

Spelling trouble?

No written manuscripts still exist for any of Shakespeare's plays. Some experts believe he wrote part of a play called *Sir Thomas More*, which was never performed or printed. If Shakespeare wrote it, he used hardly any punctuation and the word "sheriff" is spelled five different ways in five lines.

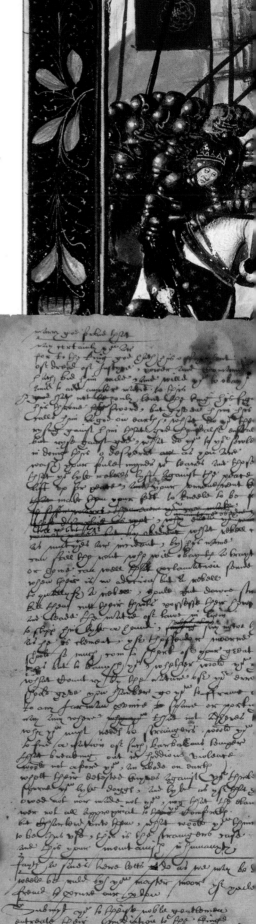

The romantic tragedy of the lovers Romeo and Juliet, from the warring Montague and Capulet families, remains one of Shakespeare's most popular plays. The first printed edition of the play in 1597 notes that it "hath been often (with great applause) played publicly".

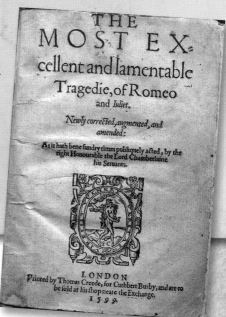

▲ Several of the history plays covered the Wars of the Roses, which had torn England apart before the final victory of Tudor King Henry VII.

▼ Romeo and Juliet *is set in the Italian city of Venice.*

First play

No one can be sure what Shakespeare's first play was but his early works were mainly histories, such as the three parts of *Henry VI*, and comedies, including *The Taming of the Shrew*. Shakespeare's first printed play, a version of the Roman tragedy *Titus Andronicus*, was published in 1594.

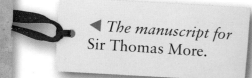

◄ *The manuscript for* Sir Thomas More.

THEATRES UNDER THREAT

Even for a successful playwright, working in the Elizabethan theatre was never easy. All new plays had to be registered with the Master of the Revels. Shakespeare would be in serious trouble if officials thought that a play would offend the Queen or other important figures.

Just as Shakespeare was making his name in the theatre, disaster struck. All theatres in the capital were shut because of a severe outbreak of plague in late 1592. Acting companies were forced to leave the city and tour the country if they wanted to make a living. Shakespeare may even have had a chance to spend time with his young family in Stratford.

▲ Marlowe may have been working for Elizabeth I's secret service when he was killed.

Christopher Marlowe

The story of Christopher Marlowe was a reminder of what could happen in the rough streets of London. Marlowe was born in the same year as Shakespeare but gained fame at a young age with plays such as *Dr Faustus*. However, in 1593, Marlowe was stabbed in a tavern quarrel. Marlowe worked as a spy as well as a playwright and this may have played a part in his death. If Shakespeare had met a similar fate in 1593, we may never have heard of him.

▼ London in 1616 as seen from south of the river Thames.

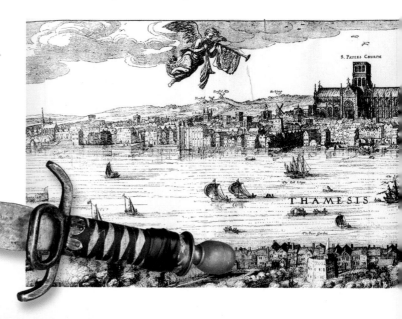

▶ Actors were trained in sword-fighting and murderous brawls were all too common.

► Thomas Kyd's *bloodthirsty* Spanish Tragedy *was one of the most popular plays of the age.*

The Spanish Tragedie:
OR,
Hieronimo is mad againe.

Containing the lamentable end of *Don Horatio*, and *Belimperia*: with the pittifull death of *Hieronimo*.

Newly corrected, amended, and enlarged with new Additions of the *Painters* part, and others, as it hath of late been divers times acted.

LONDON,
Printed by W. White, for I. White and T. Langley, and are to be fold at their Shop over against the Sarazens head without New-gate. 1615.

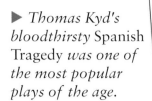

Avoiding trouble

One of the secrets of Shakespeare's success was staying out of trouble with the authorities. His rivals Ben Jonson and Thomas Kyd were both imprisoned, and Christopher Marlowe may have been assassinated.

► In 1597, Shakespeare's friend Ben Jonson was imprisoned after killing a fellow author in a duel.

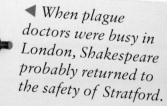

◄ When plague doctors were busy in London, Shakespeare probably returned to the safety of Stratford.

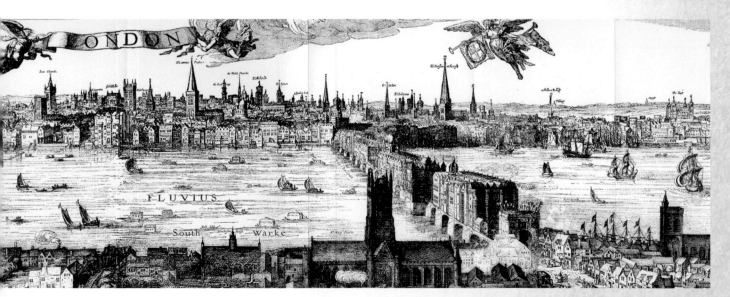

POETRY AND PATRONS

With the theatres closed, Shakespeare must have decided to branch out. Plays needed actors to perform them and theatres to stage them.

Shakespeare did not need any help to prove himself as a poet. Nowadays, most people who want to be writers think of writing a novel. In Shakespeare's time the novel had not yet been invented. Educated people were much more likely to read and write poetry. In 1593 Shakespeare published his first long poem: *Venus and Adonis*. Unlike Shakespeare's plays, long poems were written to be printed in book form. Poetry helped to make his reputation.

Seeking a patron

The people who could read poetry were more wealthy and refined than the crowds who gathered to watch Shakespeare's plays. Both books were dedicated to Henry Wriothesley, the Earl of Southampton. Wriothesley had grown up at Queen Elizabeth's court and his guardian was Lord Burghley, the Queen's chief minister.

The dedication suggested that the two men were close friends. The gushing words were not that unusual for a writer seeking the support of a patron. We certainly know that, in the years to come, Shakespeare and his plays were in demand by royalty and courtiers alike.

▶ *The area around Old St Paul's Cathedral was the centre of the London book trade.*

◀ Henry Wriothesley was still a teenager when Shakespeare dedicated *Venus and Adonis* to him.

"I know not how I shall offend in dedicating my unpolished lines to your Lordship, nor how the world will censure [criticize] me for chosing so strong a prop to support so weak a burden, ..."
Part of Shakespeare's dedication for *Venus and Adonis*, addressed to Henry Wriothesley.

◀ During the 1590s, London's printers produced just over 200 titles in English per year.

VENVS
AND ADONIS

Vilia miretur vulgus: mihi flauus Apollo
Pocula Castalia plena ministret aquæ.

LONDON
Imprinted by Richard Field, and are to be sold at the signe of the white Greyhound in Paules Church-yard.
1593.

▲ The title page of the 1593 printing of Venus and Adonis.

◀ Edmund Spenser (1552-1599) was the most famous poet of the 1590s.

SHAKESPEARE'S PEOPLE

Poetry had brought him some fame and fortune but, as soon as the theatres reopened in 1594, Shakespeare returned to his first love: writing for the stage. Writing was a solitary job, but Shakespeare must have enjoyed working with actors and sharing ideas with other playwrights. In 1594, he helped to found the Lord Chamberlain's Men, a group of actors who he worked with for the rest of his career.

Lord Chamberlain's Men

There were around eight sharers in the Lord Chamberlain's Men in 1594. They were responsible for running the company and took a share of any profits. Richard Burbage was the leading actor, playing tragic heroes such as Hamlet or King Lear. Will Kemp would have played many of the main comic parts. John Heminges managed the business, which included employing all the other actors and others required to stage plays every day.

As well as boy actors to play female parts, musicians and people to look after costumes, the company also needed scribes to write out the different parts of the play for each actor. Each theatre company performed twenty or thirty plays a year, to ensure their customers would keep coming back, so there was plenty of work for Shakespeare and other playwrights.

▲ *Richard Burbage (1567-1614) brought Shakespeare's greatest characters to life on stage.*

◀ *Shakespeare had to keep writing new plays or the customers would spend their money at rival theatres.*

Noble support

Theatre companies such as the Lord Chamberlain's Men or the Lord Admiral's Men had the support of a noble patron. This support was essential as, without it, actors could be arrested and whipped for being vagrants (someone without a home or regular work).

▲ Will Kemp was a big star of the theatre even before he started to work with Shakespeare.

In 1603, the Lord Chamberlain's Men were renamed the King's Men. Here is an account for payment after a private performance for the Spanish ambassador.

◀ Shakespeare's characters were written to suit the skills of his actors, shown here performing A Midsummer Night's Dream.

FAME AND FAMILY TRAGEDY

There are many gaps in what we know about Shakespeare's life, but we know even less of the family he left behind in Stratford. Shakespeare was regularly in contact with people in the town, but writing, performing and helping to run the Lord Chamberlain's Men would not have left much time to visit his wife and children.

The company was on tour in Kent, southeast of London, when Shakespeare received the terrible news of his son Hamnet's death. It is not clear whether he reached Stratford in time for the funeral on 11 August 1596. The loss of his only son must have had a huge impact on Shakespeare. He may have felt guilty for putting his career ahead of his family.

> "Grief fills the room up of my absent child,
> Lies in his bed, walks up and down with me,
> Puts on his pretty looks, repeats his words, ..."
>
> Was Shakespeare thinking of his own loss when he wrote these words in the play *King John*?

Moving home

In May 1597, Shakespeare made up his mind that his home was with his family in Stratford. He bought a large house, New Place, in the centre of town. The glove-maker's son had clearly tasted success in London.

If Hamnet's death had an impact on his father's writing, it was to make it even more powerful as Shakespeare produced some of his greatest work in the years that followed.

▲ New Place would have given Shakespeare a more peaceful study or library for his writing.

◀ Tudor medicine was very basic, even for a prosperous man like Shakespeare, and the death of a child was all too common.

Shakespeare's name is on this list of residents from the parish of St Helen's, Bishopsgate, London, who had not paid their taxes. This shows that Shakespeare did not own a home in London and moved regularly.

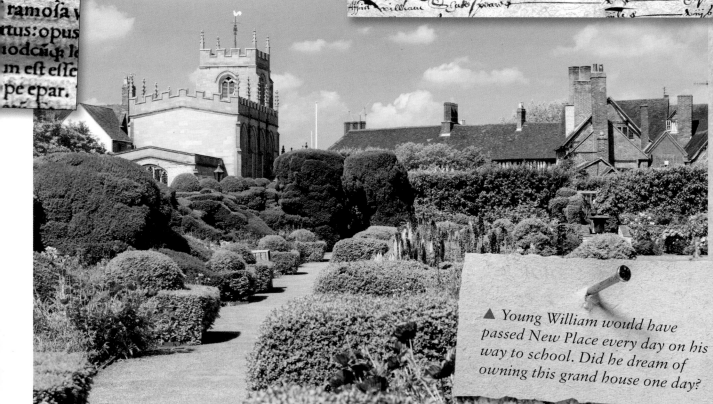

▲ Young William would have passed New Place every day on his way to school. Did he dream of owning this grand house one day?

"THE GREAT GLOBE ITSELF"

Shakespeare's plays had brought success to the Lord Chamberlain's Men but in 1598 they faced a new crisis. Richard Burbage's father James had built The Theatre, but the company had been unable to agree a new lease with the landlord. He was proposing to demolish The Theatre and the company would be without a home. Shakespeare and his colleagues could not let this happen and so decided to hatch a daring plan.

▲ The Elizabethan stage did not use much scenery or props, but cannons could be fired at key moments.

▼ This document confirms that Shakespeare and his partners were occupying the Globe Theatre in May 1599.

Burbage owned the theatre structure. On 28 December 1598, the Lord Chamberlain's Men dismantled it and carried the timbers across the frozen River Thames. They would build a new theatre of their own at Bankside: The Globe. The company would have a permanent home, but the pressure was now on for Shakespeare to produce masterpieces that would pull in the crowds.

Opening night

The Globe Theatre opened on 12 June 1599 with a performance of *Julius Caesar*. Shakespeare had a lot riding on its success, as he was part-owner of the theatre. The company had even consulted astrologers about the best day to launch their new venture. Fortunately, the play was an instant hit.

▲ The first Globe Theatre was destroyed in 1613 when a cannon set fire to the wooden building.

The risks of the new theatre were not just about money. The company wanted to open it as soon as possible, but they knew the danger of not taking care in the building. Eight people had been crushed to death when the gallery of a bear-baiting arena collapsed in 1583.

◄ This view of London from 1647 shows the Globe Theatre on the south bank of the River Thames, mistakenly labelled as a bear-baiting arena.

The Globe was now the Lord Chamberlain's Men's home, but they also performed at court and private events, as this account for payment made to John Heminges shows.

THE GENIUS OF SHAKESPEARE

▲ Shakespeare's plays often mixed high drama and rude comedy, which delighted the Elizabethan crowds.

Why are we so interested in the work of a man who lived more than 400 years ago? After all, he didn't even make up the stories for most of his plays. The language he used is very different from the way we speak and write now, and not always easy for us to understand.

Shakespeare was writing at a vital turning point in history. Theatres were staging non-religious plays for the first time. Printed books and schools enabled more people than ever before to read and write. As a result, the English language was being shaped into the language we use now, and Shakespeare was a central figure in creating this new language.

Variety

His writing has enormous variety, not just in the words he uses but also in his ability to handle comedy, high emotion and devastating tragedy. His plays and characters show learning and understanding of the world from power politics to town life. This knowledge was all wrapped up in his life and his journey from a small town to success in a big city.

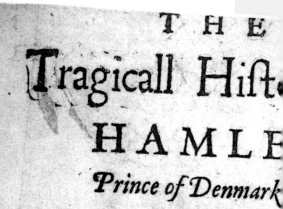

THE
Tragicall Hist
HAMLE
Prince of Denmark

By William S.

As it hath beene diuerſe times acted by h
uants in the Cittie of London : as a
niuerſities of Cambridge and Oxfor

At London printed for N.L. and Iohn
1603.

▶ Hamlet *first appeared in print in 1603, although this version was based on one of the actor's scripts and contained many errors.*

of

▲ History plays such as Henry V shared an understanding of politics that appealed to the rich and powerful as well as ordinary people.

Hamlet

(1600)

The tragedy of *Hamlet*, Prince of Denmark, is Shakespeare's longest play. The story was based on another play of the time, but the play's power lies in Shakespeare's language. The playwright used around 600 words or phrases in this play that he had never used before, far more than in any of his other works.

New words

Shakespeare used more than 2,000 words that had never been written down before. These include *horrid*, *frugal*, *excellent* and *zany*. Not all of Shakespeare's new words, or neologisms, caught on, including *undeaf* and *insultment*.

▲ Shakepeare used the English language to describe the joy and despair of lovers in some of his popular plays and poetry.

SHAKESPEARE THE MAN

There are few solid clues about Shakespeare's own personal life and character. For most of his life, we cannot be sure where he lived or how often he saw his own family.

▶ *Almost all the words Shakespeare wrote were spoken by characters in a play.*

Shakespeare must have had enormous belief in his abilities to leave home and achieve so much in London. John Aubrey, who wrote about Shakespeare long after his death, wrote that Shakespeare was "not a company-keeper", preferring to spend his time writing.

Poetic proof?

A series of sonnets that Shakespeare wrote seem very personal as they talk of bitterness, jealousy and love. The most unusual thing is that these love poems are mostly addressed to a young man. Others are addressed to a "dark lady". What we do not know is whether they are the true voice of Shakespeare, or just another character.

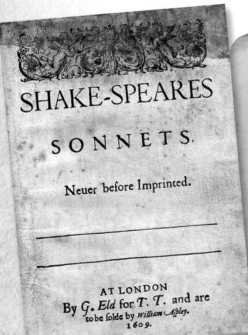

SHAKE-SPEARES

S O N N E T S.

Neuer before Imprinted.

AT LONDON
By *G. Eld* for *T. T.* and are
to be folde by *William Aspley.*
1609.

The Sonnets

(published 1609)

This is a collection of 154 sonnets, or 14-line poems, which were probably written in the 1590s or early 1600s. They may have been published without the author's approval.

Who was W H?

The sonnets were dedicated to a mysterious "Mr W H" but who was he? Some people believe this is Henry Wriothesley or William Herbert, Earl of Pembroke. However, these nobles would not normally be called "Mr". It is just as likely that the dedication was to William Hall, a printer and friend of the printer of *The Sonnets*.

There are a few documents that give us glimpses of Shakespeare's life. Here, he is named as a witness to a legal dispute between members of the Mountjoy family. Shakespeare's knowledge of the family suggests that he lived with them on Silver Street in London in 1604.

SHAKESPEARE AT COURT

The riotous surroundings of Southwark and The Globe were not really suitable for the Queen and her courtiers to visit. But Queen Elizabeth loved the theatre and the Lord Chamberlain's Men were often called upon to perform in her palaces. They also gave private performances for leading nobles.

Shakespeare, who had written many history plays about power and treachery, must have been fascinated by watching the court. The Queen's every expression or gesture was studied by her courtiers.

▶ *King James was a great supporter of the theatre.*

A new king

Shakespeare and his company gave their final performance for Elizabeth I on 2 February 1603, just a few weeks before she died. The new king was James I, who was also King James VI of Scotland. Within a few months the new king issued a warrant so the Lord Chamberlain's Men could call themselves the King's Men. There was now no doubt that they were the leading theatre company in England.

◀ *Candles were used for lighting when plays were performed at court.*

▲ *Private performances for the royal court meant that the social status of actors and writers rose quickly.*

The Merry Wives of Windsor

(1599-1600)

There is a story that this light comedy was written at the request of Queen Elizabeth. The Queen loved the comic character Falstaff, who had appeared in *Henry IV* and *Henry V*. The play was certainly performed at court.

▲ This illustration shows various characters from plays of the time, including the great comic character, Sir John Falstaff.

As one of the King's Men, Shakespeare was allowed to wear the red clothing and cloak of the royal household. According to this document, he was issued with 4 ½ yards of red cloth by the King's Master of the Great Wardrobe.

PLAYING WITH POLITICS

In Shakespeare's time, the authorities did not accept that writers should be free to write whatever they wanted. They were dangerous times, with regular plots against the Queen and the government. Any playwright who offended the Queen would find himself in the Tower of London, and many of them did.

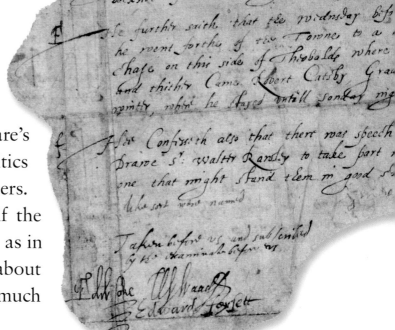

Several of Shakespeare's plays deal with politics and assassination of leaders. That was not a problem if the subject was ancient Rome, as in *Julius Caesar*, but plays about English history were much closer to home.

▲ *Anyone who criticized the monarch ran the risk of being executed for treason.*

Gunpowder Plot

In November 1605, a plot was discovered to blow up King James and Parliament, using gunpowder hidden beneath the House of Lords. The conspirators were Catholics and Robert Catesby, the plot's leader, lived near Stratford. These were dangerous times to be a Catholic. If Shakespeare did have sympathies for Catholics, now was not the time to show them.

▲ *Many Catholics were executed for links to the Gunpowder Plot, including Guy Fawkes. This is his signed confession of his part in the plot.*

▶ *Illustration from a much later edition of* Richard II.

Rebellion

In 1601, supporters of the Earl of Essex persuaded the Lord Chamberlain's Men to stage a revival of *Richard II*. The Earl of Essex was planning a rebellion against Queen Elizabeth I and his supporters asked for *Richard II* to be performed because it reflected their negative views about the Queen. The actors gave into the request and one of them, Augustine Phillips, was questioned about the political play. Below is a document from this questioning. Essex was executed and Shakespeare's patron Henry Wriothesley was sent to prison for his part in the rebellion.

▲ *Richard Devereux, Earl of Essex.*

Richard II

(1595)

Richard II was one of Shakespeare's most controversial plays at the time. King Richard had favourite nobles and no child to take on the throne after him, which was similar to Queen Elizabeth in the 1590s. A scene showing Richard being forced to leave the throne was censored and not included in early printed editions of the play.

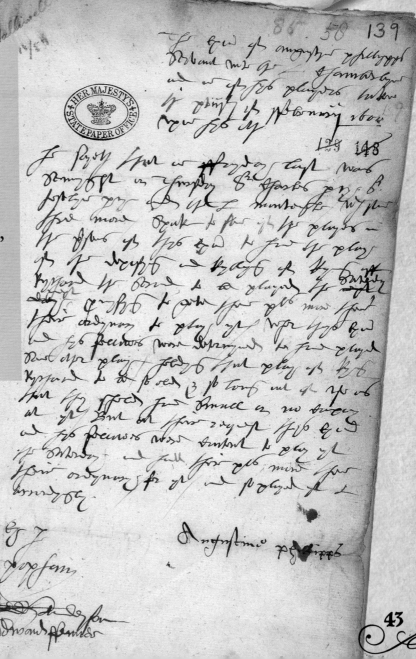

THE KING'S MEN

Rather than being caught up in the plots against King James, Shakespeare wrote plays that supported him. *Macbeth* was all about the murder of a king, and the villains were the murderer Macbeth and his wife. It showed Shakespeare's loyalty and the King showed his gratitude to the King's Men.

In the last years of Elizabeth's reign, Shakespeare's company had performed at court about three times a year. During the first ten years of James's reign they staged a play more than once a month. Actors like Richard Burbage were the best around, but it was the words of the chief writer that really got the King's Men noticed.

During these years, Shakespeare completed many of his greatest plays, including *King Lear* (1605) and *Antony and Cleopatra* (1606 or 1607). He also wrote with other playwrights, including Thomas Middleton and John Fletcher.

Moving indoors

The King's Men were a success and opened the indoor Blackfriars Theatre in 1608. Here they could charge higher prices and attract a well-to-do audience. The future must have looked bright.

▶ *The Blackfriars Theatre was the model for all the indoor theatres that followed it. Noble theatre-goers could show off by sitting on the stage.*

▼ *This warrant confirms that, from 1603, Shakespeare's company was supported by the King himself.*

▲ To perform for James I, the King's Men travelled to Westminster in west London.

▼ *The Tempest is included on a list of plays performed for the King in 1611. It was the last play that Shakespeare wrote on his own.*

Macbeth

(1606)

This tragedy based on Scottish history is one of Shakespeare's shortest plays. It was probably performed before James I. James believed that Banquo, one of the leading characters, was his ancestor. The King was also very interested in witchcraft.

Final Act

William Shakespeare died on 23 April 1616. This was close to or on his 52nd birthday, although his exact birthdate is uncertain. This was not a particularly short life in Shakespeare's time. He may have died from a fever he caught at a "merry party" thrown by rival playwright Ben Jonson.

Shakespeare had not written any new plays since around 1613. As a result, the King's Men were not as much in favour as before. They performed less often at court and the Lord Chamberlain complained that "our poets' brains and inventions are grown very dry".

By the time of his death Shakespeare was a wealthy man. He left his eldest daughter three houses in Stratford, and other property in London. His other possessions were probably detailed in a separate document that has now been lost.

▲ *At a time when everything had to be made by hand, pieces of heavy furniture such as beds were valued possessions.*

▼ *Shakespeare left some money to his younger daughter, Judith, but most of his wealth was in the various buildings he owned.*

▼ *Shakespeare was buried in Holy Trinity Church, Stratford-upon-Avon.*

Shakespeare's will

William Shakespeare's will does not contain any fine words written by the man himself, apart from three examples of his signature. Most of his property was left to his daughters Susanna and Judith. Shakespeare's wife Anne was left his second-best bed. Some experts think this is a sign of a difficult relationship between the two. However it was normal for most property to be left to the children. The second-best bed was probably the one they slept in, as the best one was reserved for guests.

▲ This scene shows Shakespeare reading Hamlet to his family.

▼ Shakespeare's death was entered on Stratford-upon-Avon's parish register. In his will, Shakespeare left £10 to the poor of his home town.

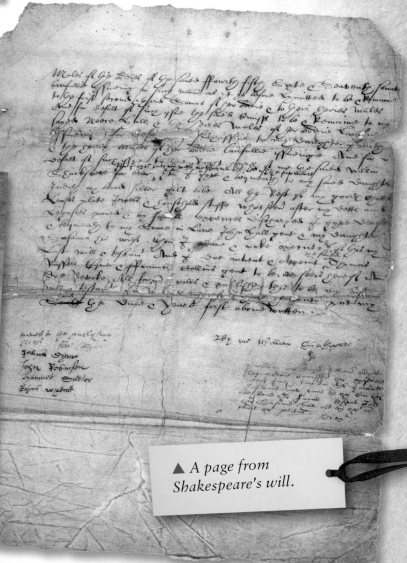

▲ A page from Shakespeare's will.

CREATING A LEGEND

In his lifetime, William Shakespeare was probably no more famous than rival playwrights such as Ben Jonson. As far as we know, Shakespeare's death was not marked with tributes from friends or admirers. Two of his fellow actors, however, were determined that Shakespeare's words would live on after his death.

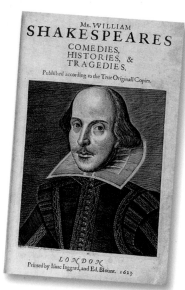

Shakespeare may have been revising his plays to get them published before he died. John Heminges and Henry Condell were the actors who collected *Mr William Shakespeare's Comedies, Histories, & Tragedies* and published them in 1623.

First Folio

This book is called the *First Folio*. 'Folio' was the size of the paper the book was printed on. The *First Folio* contains 36 plays, 18 of which were not printed anywhere else. Without the work of Heminges and Condell, these plays would have been lost forever.

▲ *There are around 250 copies of Shakespeare's* First Folio *held in libraries and collections around the world.*

Shakespeare was not always as popular as he is now. For a century after his death, the plays were rarely performed. Shakespeare's reputation recovered after 1700 and he is now recognized as one of the greatest writers in England.

▶ *Actors performing A Midsummer Night's Dream in the Victorian era.*

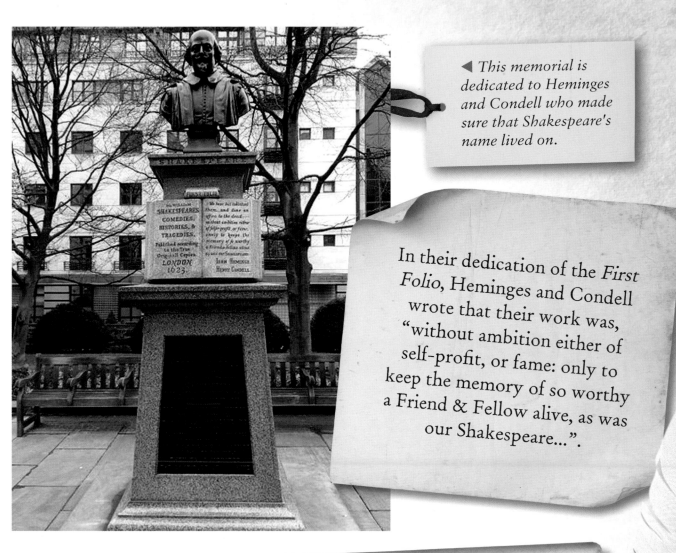

◀ *This memorial is dedicated to Heminges and Condell who made sure that Shakespeare's name lived on.*

In their dedication of the *First Folio*, Heminges and Condell wrote that their work was, "without ambition either of self-profit, or fame: only to keep the memory of so worthy a Friend & Fellow alive, as was our Shakespeare...".

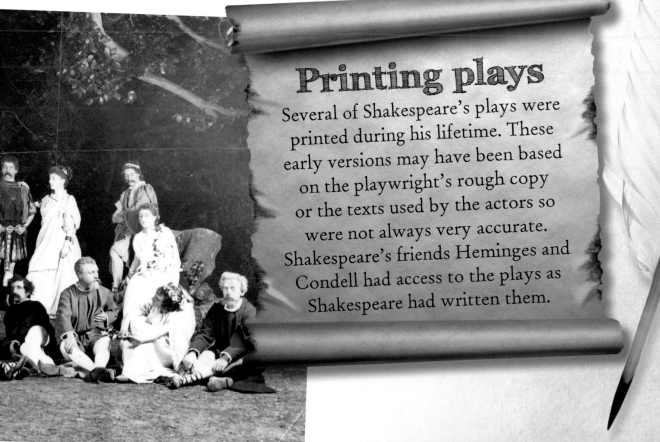

Printing plays

Several of Shakespeare's plays were printed during his lifetime. These early versions may have been based on the playwright's rough copy or the texts used by the actors so were not always very accurate. Shakespeare's friends Heminges and Condell had access to the plays as Shakespeare had written them.

WHO REALLY WROTE SHAKESPEARE'S PLAYS?

Shakespeare may have been a shadowy figure for much of his life, disappearing from historical records for years at a time. We know that a man called William Shakespeare was born in Stratford in 1564 and buried there in 1616. However, some experts have claimed that the plays and poems were actually written by someone else entirely.

These experts argue that the understanding of poetry, history and politics in the plays could not have been learned by a mere grammar-school boy from a country town. The plays must have been written by an educated man who had been involved in court politics.

▲ *The Earl of Oxford was a patron of two theatre companies and had travelled widely in Europe.*

Alias William Shakespeare

In the 1850s, American Delia Bacon travelled to England to prove that the plays had actually been written by the politician and thinker, Sir Francis Bacon. In 1918, J Thomas Looney published a book claiming that the plays were the work of Edward De Vere, the Earl of Oxford. De Vere was a poet, although it is unclear why he would publish his best work under the name of Shakespeare. He died in 1604, long before many of the plays were performed.

◀ *Francis Bacon's writing covers many subjects, but not plays or poetry.*

They are not the only candidates and it has even been claimed that Christopher Marlowe faked his own death and wrote the plays in secret. Opponents of these theories point out that there is no actual evidence that Marlowe, De Vere or anyone else wrote the plays.

One interesting fact about these theories is that no one questioned the fact that Shakespeare wrote the plays until more than 200 years after he died. Shakespeare is clearly mentioned in official documents and on plays printed during his lifetime.

The troublesome raigne and lamentable death of Edward the second, King of England: with the tragicall fall of proud Mortimer:

As it was sundrie times publiquely acted in the honourable citie of London, by the right honourable the Earle of Pembrooke his seruants.

Written by Chri. Marlow Gent.

Imprinted at London for William Iones, dwelling neere Holbourne conduit, at the signe of the Gunne. 1594.

▲ *If Marlowe was using the name Shakespeare, he must have started doing it before his supposed death in 1593.*

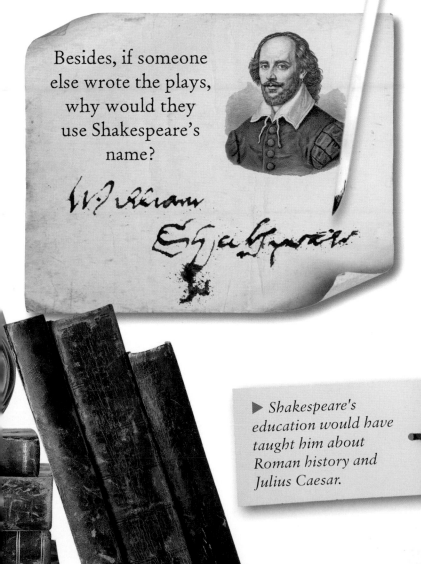

Besides, if someone else wrote the plays, why would they use Shakespeare's name?

William Shakespeare

▶ *Shakespeare's education would have taught him about Roman history and Julius Caesar.*

SEARCHING FOR SHAKESPEARE

In the four centuries since his death, scholars have tried to piece together the facts of Shakespeare's life. In total, there are around 100 documents from the playwright's lifetime that mention him or his family.

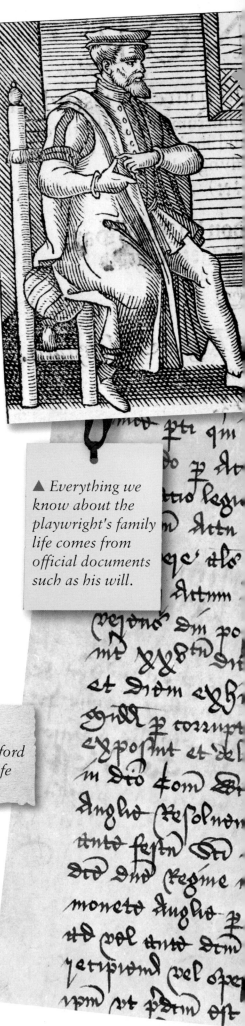

Charles and Hulda Wallace were obsessed with discovering more about Shakespeare's life. Starting in 1906, they spent years studying hundreds of thousands of documents in The National Archives, hoping to find a mention of Shakespeare. Among other things, their years of searching uncovered papers from a court case at which Shakespeare was a witness, and which he also signed (see pages 38 and 39).

▲ *Everything we know about the playwright's family life comes from official documents such as his will.*

Despite the efforts of researchers, there is still much that we will never know for sure about Shakespeare. The first accounts of his life were not written until long after his death so there are no interviews or stories from family or people who knew him.

▼ *This cottage near Stratford is where Shakespeare's wife Anne grew up.*

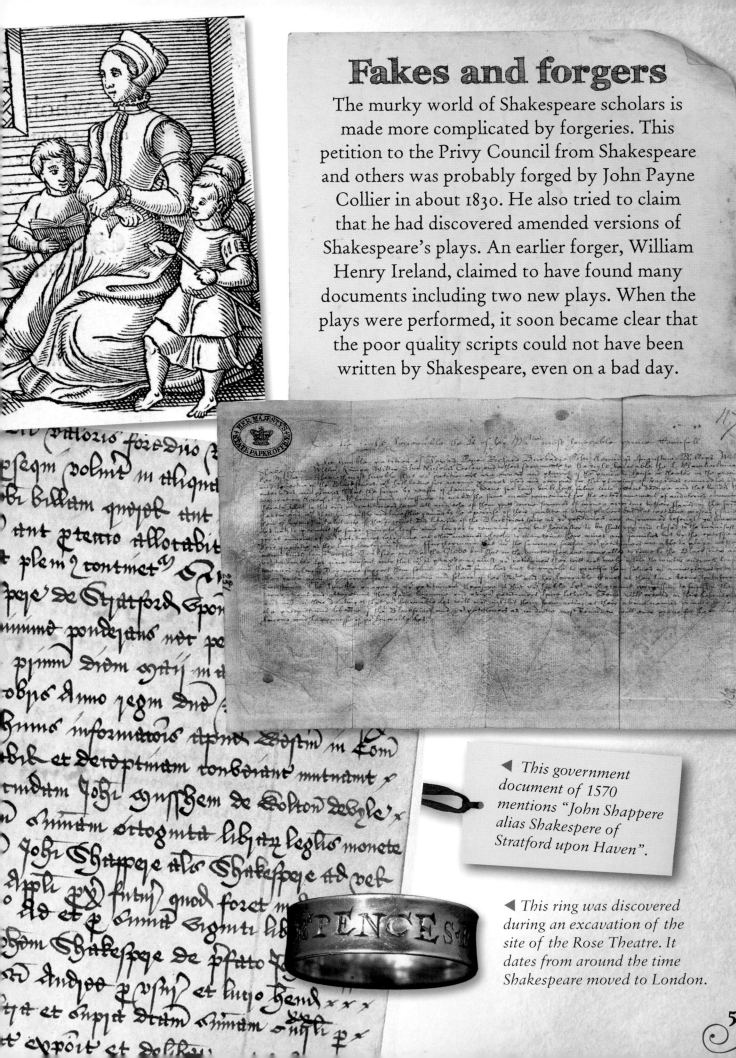

Fakes and forgers

The murky world of Shakespeare scholars is made more complicated by forgeries. This petition to the Privy Council from Shakespeare and others was probably forged by John Payne Collier in about 1830. He also tried to claim that he had discovered amended versions of Shakespeare's plays. An earlier forger, William Henry Ireland, claimed to have found many documents including two new plays. When the plays were performed, it soon became clear that the poor quality scripts could not have been written by Shakespeare, even on a bad day.

◀ This government document of 1570 mentions "John Shappere alias Shakespere of Stratford upon Haven".

◀ This ring was discovered during an excavation of the site of the Rose Theatre. It dates from around the time Shakespeare moved to London.

SHAKESPEARE TODAY

The self-taught playwright from Stratford is now more popular than ever before. His plays are performed around the world, on stage but also in film and TV versions. Visitors flock to Stratford-upon-Avon to see the house where Shakespeare was born and to watch the Royal Shakespeare Company perform his plays.

The popularity of the plays is partly due to Shakespeare's poetic skill, but they are still loved by performers and audiences because of the characters. Audiences still laugh at comic characters such as the pompous Sir John Falstaff, just as Queen Elizabeth I did. Laurence Olivier's film of *Henry V* was made to inspire Britons through the dark days of World War II. Shakespeare's words and characters still capture emotions like love, hate, revenge and doubt just as they did during his lifetime.

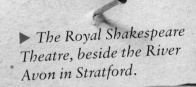

▲ *Laurence Olivier's film of* Henry V *inspired Britain when the country was threatened with invasion.*

From gloves to glory

Because we don't know every detail of Shakespeare's life, we can imagine our own version of the country boy who grew up dreaming of the big city and life on the stage. Today, we might see that ambition in the eyes of a contestant on a TV talent show. But William Shakespeare achieved much more; he was truly the everyday genius who conquered the world.

▶ *The Royal Shakespeare Theatre, beside the River Avon in Stratford.*

▶ These actors are rehearsing a battle scene from one of Shakespeare's history plays.

Tourist trouble

Not everyone was happy about Shakespeare's popularity. A vicar who owned Shakespeare's Stratford home New Place reportedly ordered the building to be demolished in 1759 because he was fed up of tourists coming to visit.

▶ Ben Jonson wrote that William Shakespeare was "not of an age but for all time". Even he may have been amazed by the enduring fame of his rival.

LOOKING FOR CLUES

Many places connected with Shakespeare have been preserved or reconstructed. Where can we go to find more clues about his life and times?

The house where Shakespeare grew up still stands on Henley Street in Stratford. Shakespeare owned the house and passed it on to his daughter Susanna when he died. Today it is decorated and furnished as a typical Tudor house, including the glover's workshop where John Shakespeare worked.

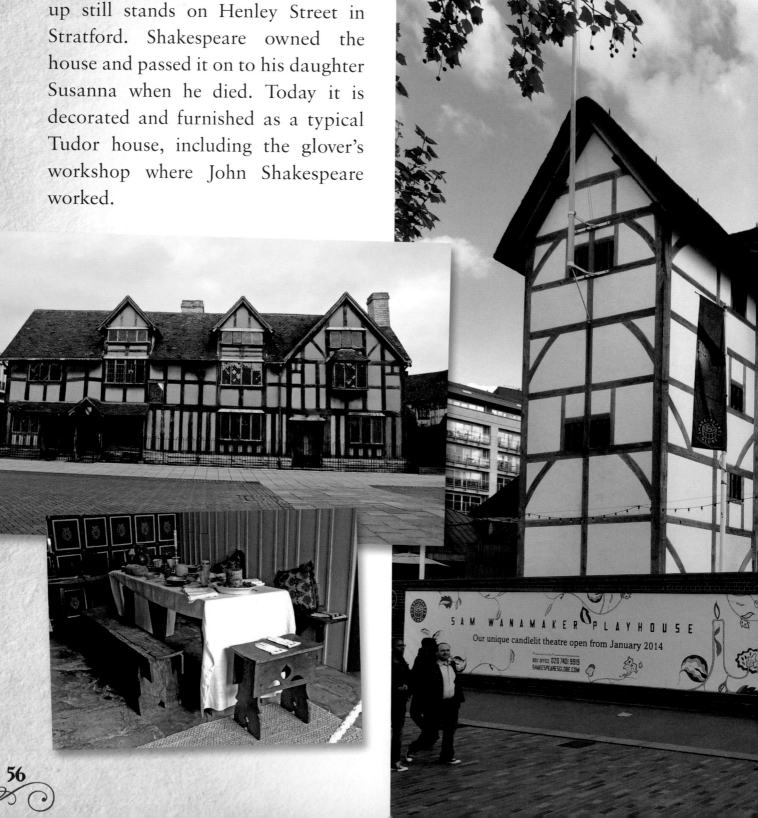

The first Globe Theatre burned down in 1613. It was rebuilt but finally demolished in 1644. The reconstructed Globe opened in 1997 as a place where audiences could watch Shakespeare's plays in a setting as close as possible to where they were first performed. The site is a short distance from where the original Globe stood, and includes a reconstruction of the indoor Blackfriars Theatre.

This monument in Holy Trinity Church, Stratford, was built by Shakespeare's family. It was probably the closest thing to a reliable likeness of him. Unfortunately, the colours in which it was originally painted have been lost.

SEASON

EVENTS AND PUBLIC TALKS
Delve deeper into the world of Jacobean theatre with our extensive public events programme.
SHAKESPEARESGLOBE.COM/EDUCATION

PUBLIC TOURS
Find out more about this remarkable building.
SHAKESPEARESGLOBE.COM/EXHIBITION

← MAIN ENTRANCE &
GLOBE SHOP
CAFE, BARS & REST

EXHIBITION & TOUR

A lucky escape
Circus-owner Phineas T Barnum tried to buy Shakespeare's Birthplace home in 1846. He wanted to put it on a wagon and exhibit it across America! Fortunately, a local committee was able to raise enough money to buy it instead.

SHAKESPEARE TIMELINE

1564
26 April Shakespeare is baptized in the parish church of Stratford-upon-Avon, Warwickshire.

1582
27 November Marriage licence issued for William Shakespeare's marriage to Anne Hathaway.

1583
William and Anne Shakespeare's first daughter Susanna is born.

1585
Twins Hamnet and Judith Shakespeare are born.

1590
Shakespeare's career as a playwright begins, probably with performance of part of the *Henry VI* trilogy of plays.

1592
London theatres are closed due to an outbreak of plague, which lasts until 1594.

1593
Publication of Shakespeare's long poem *Venus and Adonis*.

Death of Christopher Marlowe.

1594
Shakespeare is a founding member of the Lord Chamberlain's Men, the company he would work with for the rest of his career.

The first printed edition of one of Shakespeare's plays, *Titus Andronicus*, is produced.

1596
Death of Shakespeare's only son Hamnet.

1597
Shakespeare buys New Place in Stratford-upon-Avon.

1599
The Globe Theatre opens with a performance of *Julius Caesar*.

1603
The Death of Queen Elizabeth I. The new King James I issues a warrant making Shakespeare's company the King's Men.

First printing of *Hamlet*.

1606
First recorded performance of *King Lear*.

1608
The King's Men begin performing in the indoor Blackfriars Theatre.

1609
Publication of Shakespeare's *Sonnets*.

1611
First performance of *The Tempest*, probably the last play Shakespeare wrote on his own.

1613
The first Globe Theatre burns down and is rebuilt in the following year.

1616
23 April Death of William Shakespeare.

1623
Publication of the *First Folio* of Shakespeare's plays.

Glossary

assassinate kill someone for political reasons, especially a leader

astrologer someone who claims to be able to predict the future by studying the movements and positions of stars and planets

bailiff senior official in a town or district, similar to a mayor

bear-baiting entertainment popular in Shakespeare's time, in which a captive bear was attacked by dogs

blank verse unrhyming verse or poetry

Catholic a Christian who is a member of the Roman Catholic Church, led by the Pope

censor ban or change books, plays or other material that could offend people, or that criticize people in authority

comedy a play that aims to amuse the audience, usually with a happy ending

courtier someone who is a member of the household or court of a king or queen

engraving a picture carved onto a hard, flat surface so it can be printed using a printing press

financial describing anything related to money

grammar school in the 16th century, a school teaching classical languages such as Latin and ancient Greek

Latin language spoken by the Romans, and widely used across Europe in Shakespeare's time

lease agreement to rent a property

Master of the Revels an official within the royal household who was responsible for royal festivities, and also approved or censored plays in the 1500s

neologism new word or phrase that has not been used before

patron someone who supports a person or group with money or other gifts

petty school a type of primary school in Tudor England, where young children learned the basics of reading and writing

plague devastating outbreak of disease, often used to describe the bubonic plague, which killed thousands of people in Shakespeare's time

plot in a play or book, the events of the story are called the plot

Protestant Christian who is a member of any of the churches that broke away from the Roman Catholic Church in the 1500s

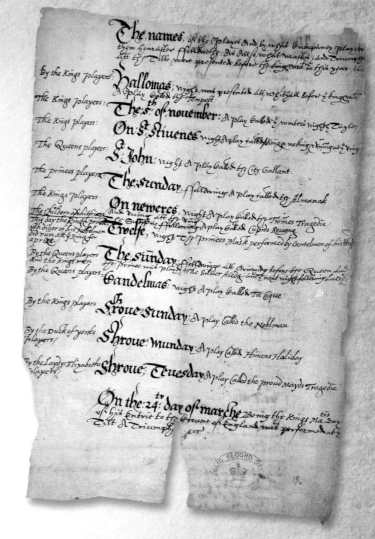

sharer someone who owns part of a business, and who is entitled to a share of any profits made

sonnet form of short poem that has 14 lines

tragedy play dealing with tragic events, usually including the downfall of a major character

vagrant someone without a home or regular work

warrant official document such as a royal warrant, which shows that a person or group has royal support

FIND OUT MORE

Books

Shakespeare by Bill Bryson (Harper Collins, 2008)
A fascinating and funny account of Shakespeare's life for older readers.

Eyewitness: Shakespeare by Peter Chrisp (DK, 2011)

Who Was William Shakespeare? by Celeste Mannis (Puffin, 2012)

Usborne History of Britain: Tudors and Stuarts by Fiona Patchett (Usborne, 2012)

Mr William Shakespeare's Plays by Marcia Williams (Walker, 2009)
Wonderful comic strips of Shakespeare's plays.

As well as the plays themselves, you can find retellings in modern English, graphic novels and much more. There are also many films and TV versions of Shakespeare's plays, and they are regularly performed at theatres around the world.

Online resources

The National Archives has created a lesson using documents from Shakespeare's life:

http://www.nationalarchives.gov.uk/education/resources/william-shakespeare/

Discover more about the reconstruction of Shakespeare's Globe Theatre in London:

http://www.shakespearesglobe.com

The best place to find out about Shakespeare's life in Stratford is the Shakespeare Birthplace Trust:

http://www.shakespeare.org.uk/home.html

The Royal Shakespeare Company website features all sorts of information on Shakespeare, including online performances:

http://www.rsc.org.uk/education/online-resources/william-shakespeare/

The National Archives

The National Archives is the UK government's official archive containing over 1,000 years of history. They give detailed guidance to government departments and the public sector on information management, and advise others about the care of historical archives.

www.nationalarchives.gov.uk

The National Archives picture acknowledgement and catalogue references

P4 Shakespeare signature PROB 1/4 (3) 3 of 3. P6 Entry of Shakespeare's baptism in parish register COPY 1/455/315. P9 John Shakespeare fined for making a refuse heap in Henley Street 1552 SC 2/207/82. P12 Elizabeth I KB 27/1289/2. P13 (top) Map of Roanoke Island, 1585 MPG 1/584. P13 (bottom) Early printed document by William Caxton E 135/6/56. P14 (middle) Richard Hathaway's will 1582 PROB 11/64 (238v) (1 of 2). P15 John Shakespeare failing to attend church for fear of process for debt SP 12/243 pt 2 f21 2d. P31 Account for payment of the King's Men to attend on the Spanish Ambassador, 1604 AO 1/388/41. P33 London Tax Commissioners listing Shakespeare among tax defaulters 1598 E 179/146/369. P35 (bottom left) Shakespeare and others occupying the Globe Playhouse 16 May 1599 C142-257 (68). P35 (bottom right) Account of payment to John Hemyngs of Kings Players for performance of a play 1603/AO 1/388/41. P39 Belott v Mountjoy William Shakespeare's deposition 1612 REQ 4/1/4/1 (1a). P40 Coram Rege Rolls, initial detail, James I KB27-1522-2 Coram Rege Rolls, initial detail, James I, 1623. P41 (bottom) Master of the Wardrobe recording the issue of red cloth to Shakespeare 1604 LC 2/4/5 (78). P42 Confession of Guy Fawkes SP 14/216 Pt1 (90v). P42 bottom Scene from Richard II COPY 1/209 (482). P43 Examination of, Augustine Phillips concerning performance of Richard II 18 February 1601 SP 12/278 (85). P44 (bottom right) Warrant for the performance of plays throughout the realm under royal patronage 1603 C 66/1608 m4. P45 (middle) Master of the Revels 1611-1612 plays performed including The Tempest AO 3/908/14 f3. P47 bottom left Shakespeare death entry, Stratford-upon-Avon Parish Register 1902 COPY 1/455/316. P47 bottom right Will of William Shakespeare p 1616 PROB 1/4 (1). P48 (bottom) Victorian cast of A Midsummer Night's Dream COPY 1/405 (370). P53 (middle) Petition by the players of Blackfriars (Shakespeare and others) to the Privy Council, to keep the theatre open (probable forgery) dated 1596 SP 12/260/117 (178). P53 (bottom) John Shappere alias Shakespere of Stratford upon Haven 1570 E 159/359 m237.

INDEX

Picture acknowledgement

Front cover: all images Shutterstock aside from the following: Signature de William Shakespeare/Connormah/Wikimedia, Anneka/Shutterstock, Stocksnapper/Shutterstock.
Back cover: all images Shutterstock aside from the following: Scott Latham/Shutterstock, Richard Burbage/Dulwich Picture Gallery/Wikimedia, Andrew Roland/Shutterstock, 360b/Shutterstock.
Inside images all Shutterstock aside from the following: p3 top right Scott Latham/Shutterstock, p4 top Georgios Kollidas/Shutterstock, p4 middle Neftali/Shutterstock, p4 bottom VILevi/Shutterstock, p5 top 464451543 Fine Art Images/Heritage Images/Getty Images, p5 bottom Imaginary_view_of_an_Elizabethan_stage/C. Walter Hodges/Wikimedia, p6 bottom 94650419 Suzanne Plunkett/Bloomberg News/Getty Images, p7 top Peter Turner Photography/Shutterstock, p7 middle Arena Photo UK/Shutterstock, p7 bottom First_Folio_VA/Wikimedia, p8 BLW_Pair_of_Embroidered_Leather_Gloves/Valerie McGlinchey/Wikimedia, p8 bottom 463917661/Hulton Archive/Getty Images, p9 top Peter Turner Photography/Shutterstock, p10 top Hornbook-Silver/Wikimedia, p10 bottom Becky Stares/Shutterstock, p11 top Francis S Walker/Wikimedia, p11 middle Alcazar_Cordoba_Roman_mosaic_06/Michel wal/Wikimedia, p11 bottom Keen_eye/Shutterstock, p12 Mayboroda/Shutterstock, p12 bottom right ChesterMysteryPlay_300dpi/Wikimedia, p13 top Capture_Of_Cacafuego/Wikimedia, p13 bottom right Dja65/Shutterstock, p14 top Alex Staroseltsev/Shutterstock, p14 bottom Anne-hathaway/Special Collections and University Archives, Colgate University Libraries/Wikimedia, p15 top Execution of Latimer and Ridley/John Foxe/Wikimedia, p15 bottom left 463917753/Hulton Archive/Getty Images, p16 171073523/Culture Club/Getty Images, p17 top IgorGolovniov/Shutterstock, p17 middle javarman/Shutterstock, p18 top sarkao/Shutterstock, p18 bottom Panoramic view of London/Wenceslaus Hollar/Wikimedia, p19 top Joris Hoefnagel/Wikimedia, p19 middle: This file comes from Wellcome Images, a website operated by Wellcome Images, a global charitable foundation based in the United Kingdom/ M0010437/Wikimedia, p19 bottom Vitalii Hulai/Shutterstock, p20 top Richard_Tarlton_Pipe_Tabor_c1580s/Wikimedia, p20 bottom Arkadi Bulva/Shutterstock, p21 top left Sponner/Shutterstock, p21 top right Swan-theatre-johannes-de-witt-ms-842-f132r-1596/Wikimedia, p22 'George_Frederick_Cooke_as_Richard_III'_by_Thomas_Sully/Wikimedia, p23 top 188006452/Universal History Archive/Getty Images, p23 bottom 109713760/Gary Lee/Starstock/Photoshot/Getty Images, p24 top 142081975/DEA Picture Library/Getty Images, p24 bottom Sir_Thomas_More_Hand_D/Wikimedia, p25 top Romeo_and_Juliet_Q2_Title_Page-2/Wikimedia, p25 bottom Juergen Faelchle/Shutterstock, p26 top Unknown 21-year old man, supposed to be Christopher Marlowe/Wikimedia, p26 bottom 1616_London_Visscher_mr/Wikimedia, p27 top Kyd-SpanishTragedie-Title/Wikimedia, p27 middle left A Plague Doctor – from Jean-Jacques Manget, Traité de la peste (1721); University of Lausanne version/Wikimedia, p27 middle right Georgios Kollidas/Shutterstock, p28 St Paul's old. From Francis Bond, Early Christian Architecture. Last book 1913/Wikimedia, p28 far left 200610210643353!Press1520/Old engraving of printing press/Wikimedia, p29 top 51243298/Hulton Archive/Getty Images, p29 middle First quarto of Venus and Adonis/Richard Field/Wikimedia, p29 bottom Georgios Kollidas/Shutterstock, p30 top Will_Kemp_Elizabethan_Clown_Jig/Wikimedia, p30 middle Richard Burbage/Ackroyd, Peter (2005). Shakespeare: The Biography/Wikimedia, p31 bottom 173276015/Culture Club/Getty Images, p32: This file comes from Wellcome Images, a website operated by Wellcome Trust, a global charitable foundation based in the United Kingdom/M0007304/Wikimedia, p33 top DCornelius/Shutterstock, p33 bottom PHB.cz (Richard Semik)/Shutterstock, p34 top Iurii Kachkovskyi/Shutterstock, p34 bottom 1647_Long_view_of_London_From_Bankside_-_Wenceslaus_Hollar/Wikimedia, p35 top 117461766/Getty Images, p36 Elnur/Shutterstock, p36 bottom Hamlet_Q1_Frontispiece_1603/Wikimedia, p37 top 360b/Shutterstock, p37 middle Sashkin/Shutterstock, p37 bottom Pavel Vakhrushev/Shutterstock, p38 416px-Sonnets1609titlepage/Wikimedia, p39 left 51246880/Stock Montage/Getty Images, p40 Aksenova Natalya/Shutterstock, p40 right 49883667/Heritage images/Getty Images, p41 Restoration_Theatre_Drolls_Characters_1662/Wikimedia, p41 bottom left zhu difeng/Shutterstock, p42 top left ID1974/Shutterstock, p43 464442123/Heritage images/Getty Images, p44 left Wyngaerde_London_-_Westminster/Wikimedia, p45 top Blackfriars_theatre_conjectural_reconstruction_1921/Wikimedia, p45 bottom 463927431/Ann Ronan Pictures/Print Collector/Getty Images, p46 top stocksolutions/Shutterstock, p46 bottom revers/Shutterstock, p46 bottom right Jane Rix/Shutterstock, p47 top 51243612/Hulton Archive/Getty Images, p48 First_Folio/Wikimedia, p49 Memorial to John Heminge and Henry Condell/Nicholas Jackson/Wikimedia, p50 top 28060691/Hulton Archive/Getty Images, p50 bottom Georgios Kollidas/Shutterstock, p50 bottom right Anna Kucherova/Shutterstock, p51 top Edward2a/Wikimedia, p51 middle Connormah/Wikimedia, p51 bottom right Andrei Nekrassov/Shutterstock, p52 bottom David Steele/Shutterstock, p54 top 162500876/Hulton Archive/Getty Images, p53 bottom 464505685/Museum of London/Heritage Images/Getty Images, p54 3171092/John Kobal Collection/Getty Images, p55 top 8022847/Cate Gillon/Getty Images, p55 middle Peter Turner Photography/Shutterstock, p55 bottom left Peter Turner Photography/Shutterstock, p55 bottom right Andrew Roland/Shutterstock, p56 top warasit phothisuk/Shutterstock, p56 bottom 481610355/Universal History Archive/Getty Images, p57 top Tom Reedy/Wikimedia, p57 left Ron Ellis/Shutterstock.